LAFITTE

THE TERROR OF THE GULF

By

Catherine Troxell Gonzalez

FIRST ED.

Copyright © 1981
By Catherine Troxell Gonzalez

Published in the United States of America
By Eakin Press, P.O. Drawer AG, Burnet, Texas 78611

ISBN 0-89015-284-5

i

INTRODUCTION

This is not an attempt to justify the acts of piracy that Jean Lafitte committed. But just as there is a little bad in the best of us, there is also a little good in the worst of us. For one brief shining moment Jean Lafitte became a patriotic citizen and fought valiantly for the United States against the British. Perhaps this little bit of good may make his acts a little less deplorable, for if the British had indeed taken Louisiana, Texas might have had a different history entirely.

I

A dull grey sky clouded over New Orleans. At any moment it seemed that the heavens would open up and flood the entire city. A young man, dressed in black clothing, stood over the grave of his young wife. Tears streamed down his face.

He shook his fist toward the threatening sky.

"My life will be spent in punishing the Spanish for this terrible thing they have done to her!" he shouted. He vowed eternal vengeance toward that hated Spanish nation.

Many stories are told about Jean Lafitte from the time he left France until he arrived in the United States. However, the truth of these stories is clouded by doubt. Nevertheless, we do know some of the facts.

In 1790 there was born in Bayonne, France, far from the shores of America, a youth who was to make his mark on the history of Texas. He became for a short period of time the self-named ruler of the Republic of Texas. This boy, Jean Lafitte, was the son of a store owner of the town of Bayonne. He grew up with a family of ten children in the south of France on a river named Adour.

Jean played with his brothers, Pierre, Jacques, An-

toine, and Mark, on the banks of the river that led westward toward the Bay of Biscay. It did not take long for the young brothers to know the magic of the sea. However, it was Jean who gazed most eagerly toward the west. His life was not very exciting up to the age of nine. But at that time he ran away from home.

His older brother Pierre had tried to talk him out of running away.

"But, Jean, where will you go?" asked the worried Pierre.

Jean had a ready answer for all his questions. "I'll just sail away where Father will never find me. I'm not going to spend my life dusting shelves in a store!"

Pierre didn't dislike having to work in the family store. It was much more to his liking than spending all his days along the seashore, like Jean. He thought Jean's ideas of owning a ship and sailing the seven seas was just a pipe dream. That could never come true. Little did he know that someday he himself would follow that same pipe dream.

It is likely that the great, busy port of Bordeaux, on the River Gironde some miles distant toward the north, was the magnet that drew Jean away from the comforts of his home town. Certainly on the river of Adour he had heard reports of the fun to be found in Bordeaux.

Jean lived very near the border of Spain and the Pyrenees mountains. He spoke both Spanish and native French. Because of the smuggling trade that went on across the border of Spain and France, Jean and his brothers often found it useful to speak both languages. Besides that, Jean's mother was Spanish by birth. So languages came easily to the brothers.

From Bordeaux the young lad shipped out on a British man-o-war. He had been on board only a short time before his father found him. The father talked Jean into returning to Bayonne. But home held no magic for the sea-struck youngster. It was only a few years before he left home again, this time for good.

Really, there seemed to be no excuse for staying in Bayonne. The family's business was falling apart after the sudden death of his father. It was time for Jean to reach out in search of his childhood dream. He would make that dream come true. He would have a ship of his very own.

Probably he went right to the port of Marseilles on the beautiful blue Mediterranean Sea. If there had been any doubt in his mind about his choice, the first view of that inky blue sea would have driven away any fears. The sea was to be his life for many years to come. As he approached the docks, he saw the tall, stately ships that were tied up alongside. He walked the full length of the busiest-looking pier. His eye was taken by the clean length of a white-painted beauty flying the British colors. On the bow under the graceful figure of a woman was painted the name "Fox."

Jean waited patiently until the work slowed down for the day. Watching his chance carefully, he slipped quietly up the gangway and ran swiftly toward the secured lifeboat. He loosened the cover and slipped underneath it. Only then did he remember that he had brought no food with him. He had only a few small biscuits in his bundle of clothes. Well, maybe it wouldn't be long until he could slip out at night and try to find something to eat. Surely the ship would sail soon. The crew had already covered the holds and secured them.

His wait wasn't long. Shipping out of Marseilles that night, the vessel rocked gently against the waves. The creaking of the winch, the flapping of a loose sail, the song of the man on watch, all served to quiet any fears he might have had about his choice. This was to be his home from now on. Even the loud curses of the seaman failed to dampen his joy. The boy had no fear. He knew that they would not throw him overboard. This ship was bound for a magic land, the West Indies, the America of his dreams.

That night he slept soundly, warm and snug under the cover of the lifeboat. When he awoke, he hungrily ate

4

a couple of the biscuits. As soon as he was certain that they were far enough from land, he crept out his hiding place, ready to face the anger of his new shipmates. Indeed, there wouldn't be much they could about him. He was on board—they were at sea—and on board he'd jolly well stay. A ship does not return to port just for a small boy.

The cabin boy, throwing out a pan of slop, saw him first.

"Lawr, heavin help us! It's a stowaway!" he shouted to his shipmates.

They all turned to stare at Jean, who made his way down the ladder, careful not to fall and embarrass himself before all the men.

"Git the old man himself! He'll probably throw this minnow overboard," called a grey-haired old man who was painting the main mast. The men all laughed and then chimed in with the other terrible things that the ship's master might do to Jean.

Jean stood his ground. He had made up his mind that they would not frighten him. He knew from the other ship that they would be rough on him. But the captain just looked at him. Charmed by the boy's handsome dark looks and earnest gaze, he ordered the cabin boy to take him to the crew's quarters. Jean followed the boy quickly. They soon had Jean squared away with a place to sleep and a box in which to put his spare clothers.

Life was not a bed of roses for the young lad. He was given the dirty chores to perform. He had to suffer the ill-temper of the boatswain, but at least they fed him well. He had a hammock to sleep in at night. His real reward came when his chores were finished for the day. He could sit out under the stars and stare at the ever-moving, ever-changing sea. The deep blue of the daytime changed to silver at night. He loved every minute of the Atlantic's different moods. Some day he'd be master of a ship like this. Everyone would work for him, and he'd be kind to the cabin boy, too.

II

Life was good for Jean for the next few weeks until the ship docked at the port of Santo Domingo. He loved the ship, and he was ready to spend the rest of his life right there on the decks of the ''Fox.'' But he was given a rude awakening. Without any discussion, he was put off the ship, alone and on his own.

''I'm sorry, boy,'' said the captain. ''Ye're just too young to do a man's work. We need men who can do the work of an able-bodied seaman, not a young splint like ye!''

The captain had other reasons, too. He did not want the responsibility of a young boy on his hands. He was not sure about the rough treatment Jean might receive from the older men. At any rate, he was anxious to be rid of the boy. So off Jean went. Jean himself felt that life wouldn't be worth living without the ship's safety.

However, Santo Domingo at that time was a good place to live. There were ripe mangoes and avocados just for the taking. A few branches of soft leaves piled up made a good bed. Jean spent his days wandering about the old city. He sat hours at the docks, watching the loading and unloading of the great ships. Here life was good to the young boy.

Before long Jean found work on a sugar plantation. During his hours of freedom, he explored the island, from the high walls of the fortress to the warm sea shore. Many of his days were spent in fishing and hunting. He climbed the old walls that ran all around the city. From these walls he could watch the ships.

Someday he would own one of those tall ships. He lay in the shade of the ugly black cannon that topped the city wall. He dreamed of giving orders to his men. His ship would sail all over the Caribbean Sea, from Santo Domingo to Vera Cruz, from new Orleans to Cartagena. He would be master of the whole sea. So his dreams ran, carrying him to every exciting port, bringing him gold and silver beyond all belief. He *would* sail his own ship. He *would* be the master of hundreds of men!

Sometimes he wandered into the town, strolling down the broad leafy avenues. He stopped to drink at the town fountain. He gazed in awe at the slave market. He read the names of the dead buried in the old Church. It was here that he met the priest who became very interested in the bright, eager youth. The priest hoped to talk Jean into becoming a priest. Jean was fascinated by the priest's knowledge. He spent many hours with the old Padre Benito, learning everything he could about history and literature. But the Church was not to be Jean's future. The lure of the sea was still too strong. His thoughts were drawn away from the old padre's teachings.

Jean did not spend all of his time with the old padre. Many happy evenings were spent in the company of other young people. There were the sons and daughters of the plantation workers. These young people enjoyed dancing and walking about the town square.

Jean fell in love in Santo Domingo. The girl was the lovely young daughter of a mill foreman. Jean took Lucia to see the padre. The old man was disappointed about

7

losing Jean from the work of the Church. However, he agreed to Jean's request that he marry them. Thus Lucia became the wife of Jean Lafitte in the great Church that both of them loved. The old priest hid his disappointment. He gave the two of them his blessing.

Jean was almost twenty at this time. He had saved his money over the years that he had worked at the plantation. Now he bought and fitted out a ship. He would carry sugar to Marseilles and Bordeaux. From there he would return by the coast of Africa to pick up a cargo of slaves to sell in America.

Jean's plan promised to be very rewarding. However, there was fighting and unrest in France about 1795. Led by the fiery Napoleon, the revolt had spread to Santo Domingo. The slaves there saw a chance to gain their own freedom. Under the leader, Toussaint L'Ouverture, they made the island unsafe for any white man, Spanish or French. Jean Lafitte had hidden his ship in a quiet bay. As soon as he could secure enough men to sail it, he took his young bride on board. They set off for safety on one of the other islands of the Caribbean, flying the flag of his native France.

Shortly after leaving Santo Domingo, they were attacked by a Spanish privateer commanded by a Senor Chevalier D'Alkala. A *privateer* is a ship of one nation that is at war with another nation. In this case Spain had given the Spanish ship the right to attack and take the goods and gold carried by a French ship. Privateering was a very good business at this time in the Caribbean. It made many a captain very rich.

That day Jean had been watching the horizon through his spyglass. The cry had gone out earlier that afternoon. The sails had been rigged for flight. However, the Spanish vessel had borne down straight upon them. At first, they had thought they could outrun it. When the fight became unavoidable, they prepared for combat. Jean's ship was not equipped to fight off the heavy cannon of the larger ship. His men were not properly trained. He cursed himself for bringing Lucia on this trip. But he could not have left her in Santo Domingo at the mercy of the rebellious slaves. They would have killed her at once.

The Spaniards signaled that they were sending a boarding party. Jean decided to give up without fighting. At least, it might cause them to spare Lucia. He would lose the ship, but with luck he might be able to save enough money to buy another before long. That is, he might if the Spanish did not kill him this time.

The Spaniards took all of the men captive. Jean and his young wife Lucia were put off their ship on a small island with only a little food and water. Unless some ship just happened to come by and see the flag which Jean had made from one of Lucia's skirts, they would die here. It was a large ocean. Even if a ship passed, their signal might not be seen. It seemed very likely that the young pair might indeed die right here.

The day time was not too bad because they found shelter in a small cave. At night they were chilled and wet. Lucia suffered from the cold. She was not as strong as Jean. Soon she was ill. Jean watched her suffering. He vowed never to stop hating the Spanish for this cruel thing they had done to his wife. His hatred grew as Lucia's fever became worse. He held his young bride in his arms and tried to warm her body with his. Just then a miracle occurred.

A passing American vessel sighted their flag. Jean carried Lucia in his arms out into the surf to meet the lifeboat that was sent to rescue them. The crewmen recognized the condition that Lucia was in. They lifted her tenderly from Jean's arm and placed her in the boat for the return trip to the ship. Jean held her in his arms as they approached the friendly vessel.

Lucia was well cared for on board the rescue ship, but

she grew steadily worse. In New Orleans the ship's crew and captain made up a purse to hire a doctor for Lucia, but it did no good. She died soon after their arrival. Jean shook his fist at the sky as he stood over her new grave. He vowed to get even for this deed.

Some time after Lucia's death, Jean Lafitte met some daring young fellows who were as brave and adventurous as he. Together they joined another vessel bound for Cartagena and Santa Marta. Lafitte would become a privateer. It was in Santa Marta that he was able to fit out a new ship. He gained a commission from Cartagena to plunder Spanish ships. He was now ready to take his revenge upon the Spanish.

It must be explained here that *privateer* and *buccaneer* or *pirate* have different meanings. A *privateer* is supposed to operate with a commission to prey upon the vessels of an enemy nation. The country which issues the commission or papers that permit the captain of a ship to attack and take enemy ships does so with the knowledge that the ''prize'' will be brought into its own ports for sale or distribution. A ''prize'' consists of the ship and its cargo.

A *buccaneer* is a pirate ship. That is, it is one which preys upon the shipping of any nation that happens to fall into its path, whether it be friend or enemy. The word *buccaneer* comes from a French word *boucan*. Boucan means ''fire made in the woods.'' It was applied to an Indian method of drying and preparing the flesh of cattle, which was used by the ships that cruised the Gulf of Mexico. Hence the foreigners who were employed in getting provisions for the ships called themselves *Boucaniers* or *Bucaneers*.

Over the years many men bore the name of *Buccaneer*. Notable among these pirates were Henry Morgan in the seventeenth century, Teach called Blackbeard, Captain Kidd, and other.

Though other loves came into Jean Lafitte's life, he

never forgot his first love, Lucia. He continued his hatred of the Spanish for as long as he lived. He sailed the Caribbean Sea in search of his enemy. When he found a Spanish ship, he boarded it, taking the prize for his men and himself. The crews he took care of according to his own whims. Most of them "walked the plank." This means simply that they were thrown into the sea to sink or swim. Sometimes they were shot, or sometimes he simply put them ashore on a deserted island. He never forgot the horrible thing that had been done to him. Sometimes the ships he took were outfitted for his own use. Sometimes they were simply sunk where they were captured. At any rate Jean Lafitte found his new business a good one. He was becoming a very rich man.

III

Just as the city of Bordeaux had drawn the young Jean Lafitte, New Orleans now served to tempt him with its charm and excitement. Many times he sailed up the Mississippi to the bend in the river that gave New Orleans its name of the "Crescent City."

One day while Lafitte was walking about town, he happened to pass a certain blacksmith ship. He entered to ask about a lodging house. He stared without belief at the young man who came to wait upon him.

"Mon Dieu"—dear God, it can't be you!" he shouted. "What are you doing here?"

The smoky black eyes of the two young men met. There was no doubt in their minds. Jean knew that this was his older brother, Pierre Lafitte. He could hardly believe his good luck. It was almost a miracle that they should meet here in this land so far from their homeland of France. Pierre had always supposed that his brother Jean had died at sea. They hugged each other excitedly.

"Jean, you old dog!" shouted Pierre. "How can this be?" There was so very much to tell. It had been a very long time since they had parted from each other.

This meeting of the two brothers happened sometime

after the purchase of the Louisiana Territory in 1803. It was a very good time for the two young brothers. They talked all morning long. They went over the things that had happened to each of them. During this long talk, Pierre proposed that Jean go into business with him. They could set up shop on the north side of St. Pierre Street, between Bourbon and Dauphine streets. Negro slaves would be hired to do the work; the two brothers would look for customers and collect bills.

Actually, Jean knew that it would be a good way for him to get rid of his "prizes." He could have Pierre act as his agent. Pierre could sell the rich goods that Jean took from the Spanish ships.

"Brother, this will indeed bring both of us great riches," Jean told his brother Pierre. "We can have all the things we used to dream about."

Pierre listened to Jean's plans with great interest. He agreed to everything Jean had to say. They formed a partnership that was to last for years.

While the brothers were talking together, two men came into the blacksmith ship. They seemed to be trying to hide. They motioned for Pierre to come with them to the back of the place. There the men spoke in whispers. They had a cargo to be delivered. They needed their horses in a hurry.

Pierre answered them with impatience. "Don't be in such a hurry. I do good work. I will not be rushed."

Jean interruped him. "Be quiet, Pierre. I think we can get the horses ready in time. I will help you."

Jean Lafitte understood well enough what kind of cargo they might have. He knew smugglers when he saw them. He motioned the men to wait in the office of the shop. There just might be a trade he could make with these smugglers.

Actually, almost everyone in New Orleans knew about the good business in smuggling. What better way to obtain at a very low price all the rich cloth, the spices, the wine, the jewels? New Orleans was a frontier town as well as a seaport. A large region, unsettled and unexplored, lay to the north and west of New Orleans. Settlers were flocking into the area. They were in constant need of supplies. It would be a very profitable business for the Lafitte brothers. Jean would see that it became a success.

Just at that moment two soldiers walked by the open door of the ship. They peered into the darkness of the place. The men in the office tried to hide in the shadows. The two soldiers walked on down the street.

"Sir," said one of the strangers to Jean, "Can you lead them away from us? I'm afraid we have attracted too much attention."

Jean looked at them, as if measuring their worth.

"I think perhaps we could help each other," he answered.

The men whispered to each other. Then one of them stepped closer to Jean. "How much do you want from us?" he asked.

"We want part of your business," answered the confidant Jean Lafitte. Pierre had joined the group in the office, and he nodded in agreement.

The men then arranged for Jean and Pierre to act as their agents in New Orleans. The profits would be divided equally among the men. At that agreement, Jean turned and walked to the door of the shop. He watched the two soldiers as they turned back down the street. Jean began talking with them. He soon had them laughing at his jokes. While they were talking, the two strangers mounted their horses and rode out the other door.

The next day the two men returned, bringing with them more details of their plans for business. Thus Jean and Pierre became members of the famed Baratarian Bay gang.

The smugglers carried on their trade by means of boats up the many bayous at the mouth of the Mississippi. There was much work for the blacksmiths. The boats needed repairs very often. It was indeed a very good business for the Brothers Lafitte. Now they would also profit from the smuggling business.

Schemer that he was, it did not take long for Jean to realize where he was needed. The place for him was on the island of Grand Terre, at the mouth of Barataria Bay. He could depend upon Pierre to run the New Orleans part of their business. He could use his full time in bringing in prizes. Jean's heart was always for the sea. He could not live away from it. He loved the great glory of the Caribbean on a warm, sunny day. Sometimes the sunsets near the mouth of the Mississippi were so wonderful he could not describe them. Jean's heart came up in his throat. He remembered one very special one he had seen recently.

About this time the United States government began a new practice which greatly aided the smugglers. One of the items smuggled became much more valuable. On January 1, 1808, the United States Congress passed a law that was to end the practice of bringing more slaves into the country. The Louisiana Territory had recently been bought. The settlers there were very much in need of help to work the large plantations they were building. They could use all the cheap slave labor they could get. They were willing to pay the smugglers to bring in slaves from Africa. The business would be very profitable to Jean and Pierre Lafitte and the other smugglers.

At first the smugglers bought their slaves from Cuba. They brought them into Barataria Bay. There the slaves could be kept in safety until buyers could come to buy them. The government of the United States was new and not well organized. There were not enough government agents to prevent the smugglers from their trade. The agents found it very difficult to control the smuggling trade. The area was large, and the force of the agents was small. The smuggler only laughed at the efforts of the agents. They could slip in and out of New Orleans right under the eyes of the agents. Many a good laugh was had at the expense of the poor agents.

Jean Lafitte saw that the slave ships bringing slaves from Africa to Cuba carried only small crews and were poorly armed. He had an idea. Their business could be improved very easily.

"Pierre, we're missing a good chance. Why should we pay the Cubans for the slaves?" asked Jean one day. "We can just "buy them" before the ships dock in Cuba. We can take a greater profit from our work."

They would simply "buy" the slaves by the use of the sword. Soon the profits were rolling in to the smugglers of Barataria Bay. And Jean delighted in making his "purchases" from a Spanish ship. He would never forget the oath he swore at Lucia's death. The thought made his work even sweeter to him.

Jean Lafitte's success at smuggling was so great that the governor of Louisiana decided to try to stop him. In September of 1810 Governor Claiborne made a public statement about the men at Barataria Bay.

"The open and daring course which is now pursued by the brigands who infest our coast," he said, "is to be deplored."

This news only served to advertise the Lafitte's business. More buyers than ever now went to Barataria in search of cheap labor. Merchants restocked their shelves with the goods that they bought from the Lafittes. Business was booming for Jean and Pierre. Grand Terre was a name on everyone's tongue.

Grand Terre island is about sixty-five miles west of the delta of the Mississippi river. The island is about five or six miles in length. The island rises from the sea with slight heights that are covered with small timber. It formed a perfect protection for the smugglers and their trade. There were plenty of fish and turtle in the waters. Wild game could be found easily on the land.

The name *Barataria* comes from the word *barratry*. Barratry has to do with naval law. It applies to any act which is of a criminal nature carried out by a captain of a

16

ship. The act is done without the consent or knowledge of the owners of the vessel. Thus *Barataria* describes a class of men, guilty of barratry, who lived on the island.

Because of the great growth of his business, Jean Lafitte decided to build a fort on the island. He intended to make himself a home there.

"Pierre, I'm going to build myself a house that will amaze everyone who sees it. I'll call it "Maison Blanche," Jean told his brother.

He built a fort near the place on Grand Terre where the Indians had erected a mound of shells and rock. Inside the wall of the fort he had his men built a very comfortable house. He furnished it with all the fine things that he had taken from captured Spanish ships. It was a place in which he could entertain all the business men who came to trade with him. Around the fort were built many houses for the seamen who came to work with him. Jean himself was the "Bos" of the entire colony. His men often called him "the old man" to each other, but to his face they called him "Bos."

IV

Jean Lafitte at this time was about six feet, two inches in height. He was slim and graceful, with dark hair and hazel eyes. Usually, he wore a mustache. His manners were those of the perfect gentleman. Ladies sighed over him. They were enchanted by his handsome good looks. However, he paid little attention to them.

Lafitte had an excellent education. He spoke Spanish, French, and English well. Most of his men could neither read nor write. Thus he found it quite easy to lead the Baratarians. As "Bos" his decisions were rarely questioned by the men. His success was amazing. He could easily handle the hundreds of men who came to work for him. These were men who would stop at nothing. They were the toughest, cruelest kind of people. Yet Jean Lafitte was their boss without any question.

Among those who came to join Lafitte was a man named Dominique You. It is possible that Jean had known him in Santo Domingo, since Dominique You was born there in the town of Port-au-Prince. Many of Jean's companions of those days in Santo Domingo came to join the smugglers at Barataria. Jean Lafitte was the opposite of what one would expect a pirate to be. However, Dominique You was almost the ideal picture of a pirate. He was a short, broad-shouldered man with fiery black eyes. He had a vicious white scar running from his temple to his chin. Despite his difference from Jean Lafitte, the two men were good friends. Dominique You became Lafitte's most trusted lieutenant.

There were others who came to work for Lafitte. One of these men was Rene Beluche. Beluche also became one of Jean Lafitte's most trusted men. Another of Lafitte's men was not quite so well liked. This man was an Italian named Gambi. Once Gambi tried to challenge Lafitte, but he soon found how strong Jean Lafitte was. Gambi was against anything that interferred with his own plans.

On one occasion the men were in a meeting to discuss which ships they would attack. Their commissions stated that they would attack only Spanish ships. Jean Lafitte reminded them of this fact. They argued angrily for hours. Gambi was interested in profits, not principles. He favored taking any ship that interested him.

"I'll have none of this," he said flatly. "I'll take any fancy ship that crosses my bow. It don't have to be Spanish for me to scuttle it."

The others tried to reason with him. But Gambi cursed and accused the others of being liars.

"I won't stay and listen to these lies. I'll take my ships away from here right now," he vowed. He left the meeting in a fury. He went outside to where his men were waiting for him. The other men left the meeting. They knew that Jean Lafitte would have to handle this mad Italian.

Jean watched the proceedings from a window. When Gambi called his men to him, Jean Lafitte walked out alone on the porch of his "Maison Blanche." He had no fear of Gambi or his men. He wore his pistol in his belt. He stood there looking coolly at the Gambi crew.

The sight of him enraged the privateers led by Gambi. Gambi stood back, waiting for some of his men to charge the fearless Lafitte. One of them, a young giant of a man, did.

19

"Aihee!" he yelled as he charged up the porch. He spat at Lafitte's feet. Bravely, he waved his own pistol. A shot rang out from the porch. The young giant fell dead at the top step. Jean stood still, his smoking pistol in his hand. He waited to see what the others would do.

They were stopped in their tracks. They knew they could not defeat a man like Lafitte. They knew that their rebellion was ended. Gambi left Barataria that day, never to return. Sometime later one of his own men murdered him.

Louis Chighizola was another Italian who became Lafitte's constant companion. He was known as "Nez Coupe" or "Short Nose" because he had lost most of his nose in a former sea battle.

Many tales have been told about "Nez Coupe." One of the most interesting is the tale of the thimble. One writer said that the story of the thimble is still told among the people who live on Grand Isle today.

On this particular day Jean Lafitte was present with a group of men. They were involved in dividing the loot from a Spanish ship.

"Now, men," Jean told the ones who were grumbling, "you know that we agreed before we set out that each of us would get a certain number of parts." What Jean meant was that they had made very definite rules for dividing the booty. Each man was to get his own fair share and no more.

"These are my parts here," Jean told the men. "Each of you gets his own number of parts. Cookie will receive one and a half parts. You know we agreed to that."

The officers had their number of parts. Some parts had been set aside for bonuses for those who were injured. Also, there were extra parts for those who had displayed special bravery. The ordinary seaman were to receive only one part. That was the cause of the grumbling. They figured that they deserved more. After all, they were the ones who did most of the fighting. But Jean would have none of their quarreling.

"We agreed before we sailed. Now take your fair share and quit your fussing. Otherwise I'll see to it that you don't even get to make the next trip," he ordered. The men stopped mumbling, took their shares, and departed.

After all the loot was divided, two Spanish gold pieces were left. Jean Lafitte gallantly offered them to the wife of "Nez Coupe."

"Here, Madam, make good use of these. Then we will not have more quarreling about how to divide them," he said.

Madame Chighizola was a very beautiful lady. She bowed deeply to Lafitte as she prepared to accept the coins. But because Lafitte knew "Nez Coupe" so well, he took the coins back. He handed them to one of the blacksmiths.

"Here, sir," he ordered. "Hammer these two gold coins into a thimble for Madame Chighizola. That way she will be sure to use them well."

He knew that Nez Coupe might just take the coins for himself otherwise.

It was indeed a strange mixture of men at Barataria in 1810. They were men whose pasts were hidden in bloody deeds. Many were French, Spanish, Italian, Portuguese, Dutch, and even a few New England Yankees. All were outlaws and as dangerous as they come. They were there for the easy money to be made in smuggling. Rich ships would provide them with plenty of goods to smuggle and a good living to boot.

From robbing slave ships to robbing lawful merchant vessels was only a short step.

"I tell you, Brother Pierre," Jean spoke, "we can make a fortune. I think we should be quick to take the chance."

"But, Jean, our letters of marque say that we can only take Spanish vessels," objected Pierre.

"Who bothers about those permits from Cartagena?" answered Jean with impatience. "You know we can make more money without worrying about the letters of marque! Let's take what we can get!''

Thus they decided to take any ship that crossed their path. However, they did take the precaution of calling themselves "privateers." They were very careful to avoid the name "pirate." A man could be hanged for that in the United States!

"Pierre, we're freebooters, privateers. We're not common pirates. Everyone knows about our business, and they also know that we are honorable men,'' Jean told Pierre. Thus perhaps they really and truly believed that they were freebooters, not pirates. However, it is more likely that Jean Lafitte did not want to be charged in court with piracy. That would go much harder for them than privateering. He chose to remain a privateer.

The wealth and power that Jean Lafitte had desired were now his. But this same wealth and power were arousing the fury of Governor William C.C. Claiborne. He was a Virginian whom President Jefferson had appointed governor of Louisiana. Despite all Clayton's efforts, the settlement of Barataria kept growing. Reports came in of American ships that were being "lost at sea." Claiborne firmly believed that this was the fault of Lafitte and his men.

Governor Claiborne spoke before the Legislature of Louisiana. "I tell you, gentlemen,'' he said, "we must get control of these smugglers. They are making a mockery of our laws. They rob every ship they meet on the high seas. The Gulf is no longer safe for American shipping, or any other shipping, for that matter. They rob and sink every ship they take.''

He finally succeeded in getting the Legislature to aid him.

"Captain Holmes,'' he told his chosen officer, "we must do everything we can to put an end to the smuggling along our coast. I know that you have only a small force, but we must do what we can.''

Captain Holmes had only forty men, but he set out in several boats to deal with Lafitte and his followers.

The news reached Lafitte long before the Holmes fleet arrived. Lafitte was highly amused. Forty men to arrest a thousand!

"Can you top this one?" he asked his trusty Dominique You. "Would everyone but a fool believe that forty men can capture a thousand good, hearty seamen?"

Dominique You replied, "Bos, I think he has a surprise coming. That Claiborne must be some kind of great fool!"

Lafitte knew how to take care of this annoying little problem. He simply had his men avoid Holmes and the small coast guard. Holmes' boat met only innocent fishermen who were bringing their catch to market. Lafitte's men just used other routes to take their smuggled goods to New Orleans. Holmes' raid on Grand Terre would have to wait. Even he knew that forty men could not defeat a thousand men.

Lafitte took the affair as a great joke. However, he was very careful to make Grand Terre safer. He added cannons taken from his ships. He would be ready for any strike the coast guard might make against him.

"Let them come now, Pierre," he said. "We're ready for them."

Holmes kept on "dogging his man." He followed many false leads. He and his crews were beginning to look a little foolish even to themselves. But on November 16, 1812, the Lafittes finally met the law.

Holmes' camp was supposed to be miles away from the route that the Lafittes were taking to New Orleans. Jean's spies had brought back that news. But the foxy Holmes surprised the smugglers headed for New Orleans with a large stock of goods. Both Jean and Pierre Lafitte were with the group. When Lafitte's boats headed across Lake Salvador to enter German Bayou, Holmes and his men caught them red-handed in the moonlight.

"We've got them, boys!" Holmes shouted in glee. "We've got them with the goods." His men answered with shouts of victory.

Twenty-nine of the Baratarians were arrested and taken to New Orleans to be placed in jail. However, Lafitte and his men were back on the streets within hours. They had immediately arranged bail. Their trial was set for November 29, 1812.

Jean and Pierre gave no thought to the cost of the bail.

"Man, look," said Pierre, "it's just a matter of paying it. We can certainly afford to lose a few thousand dollars."

They had no intention of staying in jail or of going to trial. Their little taste of jail was enough for the brothers. Their trouble with the law did not keep them from going to New Orleans, however. They were safe enough while they were on bail. They appeared on the streets of New Orleans only a few days after their recent brush with the law.

They were gentlemen, beautifully dressed. They strolled carelessly toward the government offices where they had business. They did not seem to have a care in the world. The huge cathedral shadowed them as they tipped their hats to the ladies whom they met on the square. As far as the Brothers Lafitte were concerned, life was back to normal for them.

"Pierre, this is the life for men," Jean said to his brother. He truly enjoyed the role of a gentleman as much as he enjoyed his life at sea. He tipped his hat again.

"Indeed, Jean, it is much safer than our usual life," answered the careful Pierre. He sometimes thought he would rather give up the sea for the life of a gentleman.

V

Shortly after the jail episode, Jean and Pierre with many of their fellow Baratarians, Beluche, Dominique You, Nez Coupe, and Sauvinet, their financial backer, were invited to dinner at the home of a General Humbert.

General Humbert was one of the most colorful characters of New Orleans. He had been a famous French general, but because he displeased Napoleon, he had been sent out of France. He tried to find safety in New Orleans. To drown his sorrow and disappointment with the way life had treated him, he drank too much.

The occasion of this party was General Humbert's fifty-seventh birthday. He loved the rough companionship of the Baratarians. Many of them were his buddies.

The menu that night was very fancy, the very finest of Creole cooking. It was topped off with fine Spanish wines brought in by Lafitte and his men. The guests ate until they could swallow no more.

"I tell you, Jean," spoke Beluche, "if they offer us one more course, I'll choke."

"But you'll have to confess that it's much better than what Cookie offers us on the ship," answered Jean, laughing loudly.

Finally, they were offered choice Cuban cigars. They leaned back to listen to the speeches praising the feats of General Humbert. He sat at the head of the table, a little drunker than usual.

All the fine phrases brought back the past for him. He sat in silence, soaking in the rich praise. He was becoming more sorry for himself by the minute. Finally, he pushed back his chair and rose unsteadily to his feet.

He shouted, "Your words remind me of what I was and of what I am now." He swayed drunkenly, supporting himself on the table. "I must not remain here as a part of pirates and cutthroats. My place is not here among these pirates!"

Humbert did not like Rene Beluche especially. He turned on him, calling Beluche a murderer and a thief. There was no doubt that he meant all of Lafitte's men in his statement. A cold stillness settled over the party. The men could not believe what they were hearing. Then knives were drawn from their scabbards. The Baratarians were ready to make Humbert pay for his insults.

Jean Lafitte rose quietly from his chair.

"Men, control yourselves!" he told them. The Baratarians were still angry, but they quietly put away their knives. There was order among Lafitte's crew.

General Humbert realized the mistake he had just made. He began to shake and to cry loudly. The incident was over, but never again would there be friendship between the Lafittes and General Humbert.

"Pierre, I tell you he will live to pay for that insult. I won't every forget what he has done and said to us this night," vowed Jean. It was Jean's second vow, and he still had not forgotten the vow he made about the Spanish. He was not likely to forget that he had been called a pirate in public. And it had happened in front of many whom Jean Lafitte liked and respected.

General Humbert went back to his favorite cafe the next day and proceeded to drink again. He had forgotten the events of the night before.

But Lafitte knew now that he had been branded with the name of "pirate." Perhaps he would just live up to that name. He threw himself angrily into his smuggling trade, or piracy if that's what his enemies wanted to call it. Up to this time he had somehow hoped that he could one day enter honest trade in New Orleans, marry, and become a respected citizen. But names didn't matter to Jean Lafitte any longer. Now there was no turning back. He had accepted the name of pirate in his own thinking.

Only a few days after the Humbert dinner, Jean and Pierre Lafitte were called to New Orleans for their trial for smuggling.

"Pierre, my brother," spoke Jean, "they can call us from now until Doomsday, but I'll never go on trial for smuggling. They would slap us into prison for life if they got the chance."

"You're right, Jean," answered Pierre. "We'd better not let our selves be captured."

Neither of the brothers appeared in court. They sent their business agent, Sauvinet, to appear for them.

The State's Attorney was a man named John R. Grymes. He asked the court to order Jean Lafitte to appear and answer the charges. The court was also to demand that Lafitte pay three times the value of the smuggled goods to the United States government. This payment would amount to a little more than twelve thousand dollars.

Jean did not go to answer the order. The court told him to appear, and the Marshal of Louisiana was sent to bring Jean in. This meant little to the Lafittes.

"Don't worry about it, Jean," Pierre said. "We can make that much with one rich Spanish prize. Anyway, to put you in jail, they will have to find you. That I can be sure they won't do."

"You bet your life they won't find me," answered Jean. "I know many places where I can hide from them. They'll never put me in jail again. That's impossible!"

The posters that were put up in New Orleans said,

27

"Arrest Jean Lafitte on sight!" This order meant nothing to the Baratarians. They knew that the law would never take their "Bos." They just had a good laugh over the Marshal's problem. He'd never find Jean Lafitte. This game of hide and seek went on for almost a year. In New Orleans today are found the copies of the original order, all marked "Not found in New Orleans." Jean Lafitte moved just as freely as ever, except that he had to be careful to avoid meeting the United States Marshal.

The Baratarians went on with their business as usual. They were making money hand over fist. Even the poorest seaman earned at least five hundred dollars a month. Life was good for all of them.

But Governor Claiborne was furious! Finally, he sent out a group of revenue officers to raid Lafitte's hideout at Grand Terre. The little band of officers was quickly put to rout. Lafitte's men rounded them up and took them back to "Maison Blanche." There they were entertained with much good food and drink. When Lafitte finally sent them on their way, he gave them rich presents to take back to New Orleans with them.

"But, Sir," one of them protested to Governor Claiborne, "How could we refuse? He's such a gentleman!"

Now Governor Claiborne was livid with rage. He felt that he had been betrayed by his own men. He tried very hard to find another way to stop the Lafittes.

About this time there came to the attention of the Governor the news of a sale that Lafitte intended to hold. A boatload of Negro slaves numbering almost 450 had been brought to Grand Terre. Lafitte advertised them for sale at public auction.

The smugglers had grown so bold in their work that their auctions were now publicly advertised. Handbills were drawn up announcing the slave sale. The dates were stated, and everyone was invited to attend. Jean Lafitte made this almost a social affair. These hand bills were posted all over New Orleans.

"Of course, I'm going," said one gentleman to another. "Do you think I'd miss an affair like this? There may never be this great a sale ever again in this town."

"Well, even if I don't buy anything," answered his friend, "I wouldn't miss it for the world. I love to see the Lafittes challenge old Claiborne!"

The Baratarians chose a place between Lake Salvador and German Bayou that was called the "Temple." It was a place that had been built by the Indians. Its shell mound had been used as a place for human sacrifice. The place could not be easily raided. Here the Baratarians had built sheds to house their goods. They were set for business.

This sale was a blow to Governor Claiborne. He could not stop it, and he felt helpless against the powerful Baratarians. However, he had to take some action against the smugglers.

Claiborne sent another group of customs agents to stop one of Lafitte's shipments. A fight happened when the two groups met. Lafitte killed an inspector named Stout and wounded two others.

This was too much for Claiborne. The killing of an officer could not be ignored. Claiborne would have to do something. It was then that he decided to offer a reward for Jean Lafitte's capture. Posters were put up all around New Orleans offering $500 for the capture of Jean Lafitte.

"I do solemnly warn all and singular citizens of the State against giving any kind of succor to the said Jean Lafitte and his associates...and do furthermore, in the name of the State, offer a reward of $500...to any person delivering the said Jean Lafitte to the Sheriff of the Parish of New Orleans..." the poster read. This time Governor Claiborne really meant business. He intended to get the infamous Lafitte at any cost.

Some of the important citizens of New Orleans were convinced that Claiborne would never get Lafitte.

"I tell you, sir, they can never catch that slippery Jean Lafitte," stated one gentleman.

"If they do catch him, he'll escape before daybreak," answered his friend. "They can't build a jail that will hold that man."

The people waited quietly. They wondered just what Jean Lafitte would do now. But the smugglers carried on business as usual. Jean was shown the poster, but he just looked at it and refused to say anything about it.

This excitement did not stop Jean at all. His answer to Claiborne's poster would amaze people today. It was his last dramatic act as New Orleans' most colorful figure. He had his own posters drawn up and placed all over the town. In formal language copying that of Governor Claiborne's poster, he offered his own reward of $15,000 for the capture and delivery of Governor Claiborne to Grand Terre!

New Orleans roared with laughter. It was just like that rogue Jean Lafitte.

"Who else but Jean," said one of his friends, "would think of a thing like that?"

"Well, he certainly took the wind out of Claiborne's sails," answered another gentleman.

The clever ruse had drained all the dignity from the governor's offer. It made a joke of the whole affair.

While the citizens were still laughing at the reward, Jean Lafitte with complete unconcern continued to send his stolen goods into New Orleans. There was still a very good market for the rich plunder from the Spanish ships. The Baratarians were growing very rich.

Pierre told Jean, "We have this business going our way. In a few more years we can both retire and play at being gentlemen."

"I'm not so certain any more that I would like that kind of life," answered Jean. "I like the life, but I would really miss the sea."

Claiborne was not amused by Jean's little joke, but he had too many other matters to occupy his mind. The British, who had declared war on the United States in 1812 were now readying themselves for an attack on New Orleans. That would be the first step toward taking the rich Louisiana territory for Britain.

"I tell you, gentlemen," said Governor Claiborne, "I don't want Lafitte half so much as I want to stop the confounded British. New Orleans can get over the Lafittes and the Baratarians. It's the British troops I fear right now."

However, Claiborne still had the trying Lafitte problem on his hands. He had to do something. He decided to try a new plan. This time he urged the courts to hand pick a grand jury from those people in New Orleans who did not like the Lafittes. Once the grand jury had charged the Lafittes with piracy, Claiborne wasted no time. Now he had them charged with a crime that they could not deny.

He sent his officers at once to the favorite places where the Lafittes were likely to be found. None of the Baratarians had heard about the grand jury. So they were not careful to remain out of sight. For once their spies had failed to discover Claiborne's plans.

Unhappily for the Lafittes, Pierre was captured. He was taken at once to the prison in New Orleans. There he was locked up in a small cell that was more like a dungeon than a prison. The other Baratarians escaped. They sent bail for Pierre at once, but the money was refused.

"These Lafittes don't mind losing bail money," said the sheriff. "We can't afford to let him out of jail. We'll just have to keep him until time to bring him to trial. The smugglers won't like it, but they'll just have to wait."

It was the first time that the Lafittes were unable to outwit the law. Jean did decide that his brother must have the best lawyer in New Orleans. Without any doubt that lawyer was John Grymes. It did not matter to Jean that Grymes was the United States Attorney for the State of Louisiana. His brother must have the best. He'd see to that. John Grymes would cost them money, if indeed they could get him.

"Nothing is too good for Pierre," said Jean. "I'll

move heaven and earth if I have to, but I'll get him out of that cell.''

Jean could not show his face in New Orleans now. So he sent a messenger to John Grymes. He asked Grymes to meet with him as soon as possible.

Grymes came at once to Grand Terre. The two men talked for a great length of time. Jean understood at once that it would take much money to secure Grymes' services. But he was willing to pay anything Grymes might ask. The fee for Grymes' help came to $20,000.

Still Grymes hesitated. There was something else he wanted. Jean Lafitte was willing to do anything Grymes asked. There was another fine attorney in New Orleans. Grymes did not want this man on the side of the State. He wanted Edward Livingston for his own help. Lafitte agreed to pay Livingston $20,000, also.

''I know it seems high,'' said Grymes, ''but I know that he might keep us from winning our case. We have to have him on our side.''

Jean answered, ''I don't mind the expense. Just see that you get Pierre out of that jail. I'll pay whatever he asks.''

Once again New Orleans was stunned by the actions of the Lafittes. People were divided in their opinions on the case. Most people thought that if Grymes and Livingston would take the case, the Lafittes must be innocent. Others simply said that the Lafittes were rich enough to get what they might want.

Grymes reported to Lafitte, ''It's hard, Jean. We have tried everything we can. They simply will not listen to reason.''

Pierre was kept in chains all summer in the heat of the small cell. All efforts to secure his release were useless. He became ill. The longer he remained in prison, the sicker he became. He cursed the hot days in jail. His lawyers worked on and on. They did everything they could think of to get him out. Jean Lafitte raged with fury over Pierre's fate.

"Don't the fools know that he'll die in that cell? Don't they even care?" shouted Jean. "Find some other way to work this out. We must get him out of there soon."

The lawyers hired doctors to look after Pierre. The doctors recommended that Pierre be released. In his condition he could not live. But the government was determined. They would not let Pierre go.

VI

Then on September 3, 1814, fate broke in. The men were stunned by a cannon shot just off Grand Terre.

"Bos, Bos," one of the men on the beach cried out. "They're shooting at us!"

"Man, they're coming right in," another pirate shouted.

A ship of the British fleet was anchored just off the coast of Grand Terre. They had just used the cannon shot to announce their arrival.

The pirates hurried to their posts. Lafitte ordered out his small boat manned by four men.

"Hurry, you lazy ones!" he shouted at them. "Let's get out there before they decide to come closer. Maybe we can find out what they want."

They rowed to the mouth of the inlet. The men were trying to see the ship.

"Look, Bos, they're flying the British colors," shouted the first man, pointing toward the brigantine.

"I see, I see," answered Lafitte impatiently. "What on earth can they want of us?"

As soon as the ship's crew saw Lafitte's boat, a small gig shot out from the side of the brig. It contained two naval officers and an army officer.

Placing his hands to his mouth, Lafitte called to the gig, "State your business before you come closer."

Captain Lockyear answered Lafitte's challenge. "We want to see your Mr. Lafitte." The gig carried a white flag of truce. They could see that now. Still Jean did not give his presence away. He waved toward the shore.

"Pull on in. You may see him there," he shouted back.

The British gig followed Lafitte's boat in toward the shore. Lafitte waited until the two boats were beached before he let the men know who he was.

"Bos, don't let them traitors in here!" shouted one of the pirates. "Spies ain't welcome here."

"Let's show them traitors what they've gotten themselves into," cried another tough-looking thug. "Let's get 'em, boys!"

Jean had to quiet his men, who were ready to arrest the "spies." He led the visitors through the group of grumbling men. They went into Maison Blanche, where Lafitte welcomed them graciously and invited them to take refreshments with him. The British officers were treated royally. They tried to state the purpose of their visit, but Lafitte insisted upon eating and drinking first. He always treated his guests with the proper courtesy.

"First, gentlmen, let me give you some of this good Madeira. I assure you it is the very best wine to be found," said Jean. Cold roast fowl and good fresh hot breads were brought in at once, as though they had been expecting guests. Fine Cuban cigars finished the repast.

Finally, Jean settled back and showed them that he was ready to hear them out. One of the gentlemen handed him a package containing a letter to him and two notices to the Louisianans. Jean turned the package over and over in his hands before he tore the wrapping off. The seals, as he broke them, were imposing and official looking. Jean wondered, as he started to read, what they could have to do with a pirate.

35

One paper was a statement from the British government calling upon all people of Louisiana to join the British against the Americans.

One of the officers stopped Lafitte's reading of the papers.

"Sir, we need your help. You are in a perfect position to help us in our attack on New Orleans. You know all the bayous and lakes that lay between here and the city," said the naval officer.

"That we do," agreed Jean Lafitte. "We know them as well as you know the back of your hand. But I'm not sure that we want to help you. We have our own work to do. I'm sure you know that we run a profitable business here on Grand Terre?"

"Indeed, we do, sir," answered the other naval officer. "But surely you can put off your work for a short time?"

"Sir, seriously," said the army officer, "we have made offers to you and your men that I am certain you will find quite interesting."

As the officer said, the letter did indeed offer many things to the Lafittes. First, Lafitte was to be made captain of a British frigate. Then he would receive $30,000 in cash. Also, he and his men would receive land from the British. Finally, the British would aid in freeing Pierre.

This last offer was tempting, to be sure. Jean listened to Captain Lockyear's plans as he talked about the good that the pirates would gain. Jean held back any show of feeling. He folded the letters carefully. He put them in his breast pocket.

"Your plan seems almost perfect," Jean said to Lockyear. "I cannot give you my answer just now. I need to talk with my men. They are not all here. It will take about two weeks for me to discuss it with all of them. Then I will give you my decision."

"That is fine, sir," said the naval officer. "We will be back here in exactly two weeks. In the meantime we will remain on our ship out in the Gulf."

Jean stalked out of the house after the men were out of sight upon the water.

"Don't these fools know that I have my own fleet?" stormed Jean. "And they offer me a captain's place on one frigate?"

"Better yet," shouted Dominique You, "they want to give you the wealth that we can take from one of their ships. Just from one ship! What fools they must think us!"

"Well, I want Pierre out of that jail, but I can think of a much better way to get him out now," answered Jean. The laughing men shouted and clapped each other on the shoulders.

"We'll slip Brother Pierre right out of that cell," cried one of the pirates.

"No, I have a plan," said Jean. Indeed he did have a better plan up his sleeve. He sent Dominique You with the letters the next day. Dominique You was to deliver them to one Jean Blanque, a friend of Lafitte's who was serving in the Louisiana State Legislature.

In his own letter to Jean Blanque, Jean Lafitte said that although he might have failed pay duties on some of his goods that he had brought into the country, he had never ceased to be a good citizen. He spoke of his brother Pierre whom the British had promised to free. He also told of his worry about Pierre's illness.

"I fear that our country will be invaded by the British. New Orleans lies open to their forces unless more men can be stationed there. An invasion of the Louisiana Territory might very well succeed right now," Jean said. "It is necessary that some steps be taken to protect the city of New Orleans."

Whatever effect Jean's letter may have had upon Jean Blanque, it is certain that another surprise was in store for the officials in New Orleans. That very night Pierre Lafitte managed to escape from the thick-walled, windowless dungeon in which he was imprisoned. He made his way back to Grand Terre as soon as he could.

"Pierre, is it really you? You're so pale. Thank God, you're free!" spoke Jean Lafitte upon seeing the thin, pale form of his brother.

"I hope to God that I never have to spend time in that place again," replied Pierre. "I'm so cold that I'll never get warm again. Even in the heat of the summer, I felt cold in there." His fever had left him shaking and weak.

Five days later, Jean Lafitte offered the services of himself and his men to Governor Claiborne. Pierre's freedom had taken away the only hold the British might have had over Jean Lafitte. Now he could answer the British the way he had wanted to answer them from the very first day.

To Governor Claiborne, Jean detailed the British proposal. "They want us to lead them through the swamps and bayous to New Orleans," wrote Jean. "I have never ceased to be a loyal citizen of the United States. How can I lead the British against my country? I may have failed to pay duty on some of the goods at times, but I am a citizen. All that my men and I ask is that our rights as citizens be given back to us. We will make as patriotic citizens as any in the United States. We want to fight for our country."

Lafitte's offer was considered by a committee of citizens meeting with Governor Claiborne.

"I tell you, gentlemen," said Commodore Patterson of the Navy. "I do not trust these outlaws. They will turn on us without cause."

"I'm with you, Commodore," answered Colonal Ross of the United States Army. "Indeed we would be unwise to trust this kind of man."

"But, men," interrupted Governor Claiborne, "we do not have enough men stationed here to hold off an attack by the British. They will murder us. Our women and children are in great danger every moment we delay. Dare we refuse this help that might save the city?"

Lafitte's offer was refused. Patterson and Ross voted

Claiborne down. They felt that they could take care of the pirates. The two men had been arming their forces for an attack on Barataria. They wanted to destroy the pirate stronghold.

Ross said, "That will be much better than having a bunch of blood-thirsty pirates fighting side by side with our good, God-fearing troops!"

"We must rid our country of this danger to our commerce," added Patterson.

The expedition under Commodore Patterson attacked the stronghold at Barataria on September 16, 1814. When the ships came in sight of the island, the pirates were ready for them. At first the pirates thought that the ships were the British returning.

Cannons were placed in position for a fight. All the barricades were manned by pirates ready for a signal from their leader.

"Bos, that's not a British ship," shouted one of the men out on the point. "That's an American flag they're showing. Do you think they're trying to trick us?"

When the smugglers saw the American colors, they did not resist. Some of the pirates on board the schooner, "The Lady of the Gulf," ran up a white flag of truce. There wasn't a man there willing to fight against the American flag. Jean Lafitte had said that he would never fire a shot against the flag of the United States. The pirates just quietly disappeared from the island and the ships. They knew the swamps so well that they were out of sight before the American ships could land an attack force. Only a few of the pirates were captured. Lafitte was not found.

The Americans captured six schooners, a brig, and a felucca that were without flags, and the two schooners that were flying the Cartagenian flag. The entire pirate settlement was burned to the ground. The Lafittes went into hiding on the coast. They knew these marshes like a second home.

"I tell you, Pierre," said Jean Lafitte, "I know that

they need us. I still think I can persuade Governor Claiborne to pardon us and let us serve our nation."

"Well, Jean, you may be right," answered his brother. "But you know how stubborn that fool Patterson can be. He will talk Claiborne out of helping us. Look what he did at Grand Terre. It's gone, every stick of it."

"I know, my brother. Nevertheless, we must try. If we don't, the British will take Louisiana," reasoned Jean. "I'm going to try again to convince Claiborne."

He sent a message urging the importance of his offer to help in the defense of New Orleans. He spoke of the lack of troops to defend the city. He tried to explain the feeling that his men had for the United States. After all, had they not refused to fight against Patterson and his forces at Barataria?

When General Andrew Jackson rode into New Orleans, he was dismayed at the lack of troops. Ill and drawn, he faced an almost impossible challenge. But he was against having the Lafittes under his command. He called them "these hellish banditti."

He insisted, "I will not call upon pirates and robbers to join in our glorious cause. The United States does not need these bandits."

However, the battle drew closer. Jackson had only a force of about twelve hundred men. The British forces were twelve thousand strong. Jackson thought again about Lafitte's pirates. He was already drilling the Negroes and Indians, and he had ordered the jails opened for more men.

Then came the fact that changed Jackson's mind about the Lafittes. A shortage of flints for their guns hampered the soldiers of General Jackson.

"Governor, I tell you the truth. We cannot win this battle unless we can get the flints that we need," the general told Claiborne. "We won't even have a chance against the British."

"Well, General Jackson, as I said before," began

Governor Claiborne, "the pirates are ready and willing to help."

Secretly the governor sent word to Jean Lafitte to come in to his office for a conference. He knew that Lafitte would move heaven and earth to please the general. Without the flints, the guns were useless. Perhaps Lafitte would have an answer for the problem. When Lafitte learned of the shortage of flints, he was delighted.

"Sir, you will be pleased to know that I know where I can get seventy-five hundred flints, if they will help," said Jean happily. He knew he had won his cause.

This would be his chance to persuade General Jackson that he and his men should be pardoned and allowed to serve the United States.

"Lafitte, sir," the Governor said, "I can assure you that the General will be very happy to see you today."

Now Livingston came to the aid of the Lafittes. He was a friend of the General. He reminded Jackson of the Lafittes' offer to help. Thus Jean's offer of the flints settled the question.

General Jackson used his power during war time to pardon the smugglers. Governor Claiborne invited the Baratarians to join the cause. They now had a full and free pardon. They came running to join the army. Some seventy or eighty of them were freed from prison to fight. Overnight the name of Jean and Pierre Lafitte was changed from that of "pirate" to that of "patriot."

From this time on, Jackson talked about the Baratarians as "these privateers" instead of talking about "those hellish banditti." Jean Lafitte was prouder of being a citizen of the United States than he was of the change in fortunes. He was now Jean Lafitte, Patriot!

Three men rode into New Orleans, their horses' mouths covered with foam. They had ridden full speed from the south. It was the morning of December 23, 1814, only two days before Christmas. The town was getting ready for the holidays. But the news was too frightening.

The first of the British troops were camped only nine miles down the river on the Villere plantation.

"Governor, there are twelve thousand of them, at least that many," said Villere. "We came as soon as we could."

"Can you tell me anything about their arms?" asked General Jackson. "It would help to know how well they are armed."

"Sir, we didn't stay there long enough for that," answered the second man. "We felt that we needed to warn you."

"I thank you, gentlemen," said General Jackson. "We need all the help we can get in these dangerous days. Governor, I will issue a call at once for a review of the troops. We have work to do!" He turned to the governor with these last words.

By now General Jackson had two thousand, one hundred and thirty-one men at his service. With these few, he must save New Orleans.

"Our chances are slim, gentlemen. We must do the very best we can. I have a plan that will help," Jackson said to his aides.

He had decided upon a plan that might save New Orleans. He would surprise the British with a sudden attack. The general was right in his thinking.

The British were stunned by the attack. "He must have thousands of men in reserve. Only a fool would attack with that rag-tag army," said the British general.

The British could not believe that this ragged army was all that Jackson had. They were certain that there must be thousands of mad Americans awaiting them in New Orleans.

"Sir, our spies have not located their troops," said an aide to the British general. "They must be stationed outside the city. We have looked the entire city over, and there are no more troops in that city!"

"Well, General Jackson is a shrewd old man. He

would not let us know his strength," answered the British officer. "We'll have to chance it, anyway. After all, we have thousands of men in reserve."

The Battle of New Orleans took place two weeks later on January 8, 1815, but it was the first battle that really saved Louisiana. It was a stroke of genius that allowed General Jackson to bluff the British. Or perhaps it was as the British leader had said. Jackson was a shrewd old man. He knew his battle strategy.

Jackson now had time to prepare. He secured two thousand reinforcements and got ready for the attack that he knew would come soon.

The war did not disturb the Baratarians. They looked forward with pleasure to the fighting.

"Dominique," said Pierre Lafitte, "you like this better than you do a sea fight, I do believe."

"I do. I do, my friend," answered Dominique happily. He spat on his knife as he worked to sharpen it. It couldn't come too soon to suit him.

Just before the attack came, General Jackson happened upon a group of the Baratarians making coffee for their breakfast.

"That coffee smells better than anything I have smelled lately," said the general. "Is it smuggled in from Cuba?"

"It is, my general, it is," answered Beluche. "We brought it in just for you." They all roared loudly at this joke. General Jackson laughed with them. He stopped to drink a cup of their coffee before riding on down the camp.

Beluche and Dominique You were in charge of cannon facing the enemy. They had able men working with them. Pierre Lafitte was also fighting on land. But Jean Lafitte was sent aboard a vessel to guard against an attack from the Gulf. He was stationed near the Temple because he knew the area so well.

Later on he was seen fighting at Chalmette. All the

43

Baratarians were right in the middle of the fighting. After the battle was over, General Jackson had nothing but praise for the brave men. In fact, he now referred to them as "these gentlemen." No longer did he call them pirates.

"I would rather have these men," he said, "than all the troops the British brought to oppose us."

On January 23, 1815, New Orleans celebrated the victory. Everywhere there were decorations.

"Have you seen the square in front of the Church?" asked Jean. "Pierre, they have more flags and bunting than you ever saw."

"Well, I saw the priests," answered Pierre. "Jean, they have on all their silks and satins. You must see them!"

Everyone was in a mood of joyous happiness. New Orleans had been saved. The man whose name was on every lady's lips was Jean Lafitte. It was almost as though he had done it alone. They spoke of his dark, handsome good looks. They liked his courteous manners and easy way of speaking. He was the hero of the moment.

The crowd filled the square before the Church of St. Louis. When General Jackson appeared, the crowd went wild with shouting. That night there was a ball at the French Exchange. There was dancing and a tremendous supper for all.

"Have you seen him?" asked one pretty young lady.

"No, but I know that he is here," answered her companion.

"Let's look in the dining room. He must be there because I can hear all the voices," said the first young lady.

They hurried into the other room. All the ladies were anxious to see Jean Lafitte. They had heard so many different stories about him. They were fascinated by the legend of the Lafittes. Strange as it may seem though, no one had any comment to make about Pierre. Perhaps he was not so appealing to the ladies. Pierre apparently paid little attention to them. Jean, on the other hand, told a different story about his past to each lady. He kept their attention. They loved his stories, even though they did not believe all of them.

"He told me that the Spanish caused the death of his first wife," said one lady.

"But he said that he had never been married," argued her friend.

"I think he is really in love with a Creole lady," added another of the crowd of ladies.

Jean Lafitte was a very romantic figure to the ladies of New Orleans. The deep, dark secrets of his past stirred their imaginations as nothing else had ever done.

VII

Despite his popularity on this festive night, the ladies of New Orleans never saw him again. Jean Lafitte had laughed and talked with Governor Claiborne. They had joked about the rewards that they had posted. But soon their gay groups was joined by one who was not quite so happy. Brigadier-General Coffee walked up. He knew most of them, but he hesitated to hold out his hand to Jean. Perhaps Coffee was only trying to place Lafitte in his memory. However, his hesitation caused Jean to assume that Coffee intended to insult him. He stepped closer to Coffee and said furiously, "Lafitte, the Pirate!"

At these angry words a hush fell over the room. They had never seen Jean Lafitte in such a mood. His men knew his anger. They tensed as though expecting a fight.

General Coffee apologized at once.

"I'm sorry, Lafitte. No injury was intended," said Coffee. He had not intended to insult Lafitte. The shock of the moment almost frightened Coffee. The angry looks of the Baratarians left him cold.

Jean Lafitte and General Coffee shook hands. But those who heard the talk would never forget Lafitte's fury. They would remember the hatred for a long time.

Lafitte did not forget it either. That night he spoke to Pierre about it.

"I tell you, Pierre, that pompous popinjay need not think he can treat a Lafitte that way," said Jean, shaking his head in anger.

"He might find he has opened his mouth once too often," answered Pierre. "I could have gladly run him through with my good sword."

"Well, Pierre, there will come another time. We'll just bide our time," answered his brother. "When we meet again, perhaps the ladies will not be present."

"Ay, ay, brother," answered Pierre. He agreed with Jean that General Coffee should beware of the Lafittes in the future.

Jean and Pierre began their requests to President Madison for the pardons that had been promised them. They wanted a full pardon by the United States government. President Madison did not waste any time. On February 6, 1815, he issued a lengthy statement, giving all the reasons that the Lafittes should have their pardons. He spoke of their actions at the Battle of New Orleans. For these reasons, Madison issued a full pardon for all the men from Barataria. It now seemed that Jean and Pierre Lafitte could begin their new lives as honest and respected business men and citizens. Madison's kind words sweetened the memory of Coffee's insult.

But unfortunately, there was more to consider. Jean Lafitte was not satisfied.

"Pierre, we need our ships. The government must return them to us. The pardon is not enough," said Jean to Pierre. "We cannot go on. Our whole life is mixed up. Barataria has been destroyed. I tell you, Brother Pierre, we must make them give us back our ships!"

"Jean, you go to Washington. Perhaps you can convince Madison that they owe us that much," answered Pierre.

"While I'm there, Pierre," said Jean, "you round up

the men. Get them to join us here. We'll find another base for our operations. Tell them to be ready to leave at once."

He would settle his problem with the government. He just wanted his own property back. The government had taken it from him. He did not consider how he had gotten it in the first place. To Lafitte, the commission from Cartagena made it all legal.

The two lawyers, Grymes and Livingston, started a suit in the United States courts to get back the ships and goods. Jean Lafitte spent weeks in Washington. He talked with everyone he could about his ships. He went everywhere. He was invited into many homes. Everyone had heard of this man Lafitte. They were all delighted to entertain him. It gave them a certain pleasure to have a pirate in their homes. They could talk about it to their friends. Jean spent almost sixty thousand dollars. The invitations he had accepted must be repaid.

"Jean," said Pierre upon one visit to his brother, "you are spending us blind. We'll have nothing left."

"But, Pierre, we must keep up with society. These people are important to us," answered Jean. "I need the contacts. I am making progress."

Unfortunately, in New Orleans his efforts were not liked. He was left open to criticism. His critics demanded to know why he still continued to go to Grand Terre. If he had truly changed, why were the Baratarians still there? His patriotic efforts were dimmed by this talk. People were suspicious of him now.

And in Washington, Lafitte was destined for disappointment. With the suits facing the government, the officials settled the matter. The government put the vessels up for public auction. That would get the property out of Lafitte's hands for good.

But the Lafittes had another ace up their sleeves. The vessels were bought, but it was Sauvinet who purchased them. Sauvinet was still serving the Lafittes. It was really their own money that paid for the ships. Now their problems were solved. Jean and Pierre Lafitte still possess great wealth, and now they had a fleet of ships. All it took was for Sauvinet to transfer the ownership of the vessels to the Lafittes.

"We've made it, Pierre," shouted Jean. "We're back in business! As soon as they can be fitted out, we'll start looking for a new base."

"Indeed we are," answered the excited Pierre. "We can go back to sea now. I can't wait to get back to the old life."

The old business would not be the same, however. The United States had opened diplomatic relations with both Spain and England. Now there was no way that the Lafittes could be defeated again. They were back in the life of the sea.

"Pierre, they can call us what they like now," said Jean. "I don't care any longer what they say about us."

VIII

The Gulf of Mexico and its shores still had charms for Lafitte. He went to Baltimore, Maryland, to have his vessels outfitted. Then he sailed to Central America to try to get new papers for privateering. From these newly formed governments he might get the right to prey upon the shipping of their enemy nations. Then the pirates would be free to do as they pleased.

"Jean, what about going to Port-au-Prince?" suggested Pierre. "We might find a good base there. You know that we both like the warm weather and the sunshine we'll find there."

"Ay, ay, Pierre," said Jean. "Indeed we do like the sunshine. I dislike leaving New Orleans, but it looks as though we're out of business here. There's nothing we can do about it."

"Then let's make our way to Haiti as soon as possible. We can find a good secluded bay and set up business again," answered Pierre. "All we have to do is to find a few good prizes. Then we're back at the old trade."

"You're right, Brother," said Jean. "I'll be happy to be back at sea again. I've had too much of Washington already. I don't ever want to go back there." His efforts there had been in vain. He felt that the people he met were vain. They didn't really like him. They only enjoyed the money he had spent.

The brothers took their newly fitted vessels, their old Baratarian friends, and enough provisions to last them for a couple of months. They set sail for Port-au-Prince. They had left many friends there in former years.

"Jean, I know Jacques will be glad to see us," said Pierre.

"Of course, Pierre," said Jean happily. He too thought that they would be welcomed in Haiti.

But they were wrong. Their reputations had gone before them. They were not welcome in Haiti. They were met by persons they did not know.

"Sorry, gentlemen," said these authorities. "You may take on provisions, but you must leave this port at once."

"Come on, Pierre," ordered Jean. "This is not the only spot in the Caribbean. It's a big place. We can still find a good base here."

The brothers were disappointed. However, they did not let this defeat stop them. At once they started looking about for another spot.

"Jean, you remember what Jim Campbell said about Texas," Pierre reminded Jean. "The coast is not settled. Both the Spanish and the English still claim it. It should be an ideal place. We won't be bound by the laws of either country."

"We can find a quiet bay to build our new homes," answered Jean. "We'll have a new start there. We won't be bothered too much by the law."

At this time there was an uninhabited island, a long narrow body of land stretching along the coast of Texas. It was called "Snake Island." Along the edge that guarded the bay was "Punta Culebra" or Snake Point. Some years before Commodore D'Aure had secured a commission from the Mexican Revolutionists. He had taken possession of the island of Galveston as the Governor of Texas.

"You remember, Pierre," said Jean. "Bill Cochrane told us about the good harbor they found there."

Pierre answered, "I know that we have several men who have lived on the island. They didn't care much for D'Aure, the harbor was good and plenty deep. There is a bar, Campbell said, over the entrance. That would just serve to keep out those we don't want. We could patrol it at times when we fear trouble."

"Sounds like just what we're looking for," interrupted Jean. "Let's go there and see for ourselves."

The men who had lived there under D'Aure encouraged Jean and Piere in their plans. They were very excited about the idea. It seemed that Texas would be the answer to their problems.

The pirate fleet put in to the Island in due time. The place was about thirty miles long and about two miles wide in the center with only a few clumps of trees. There was rank grass growing almost to the edge of the shore. The entire island was covered with thousands of snakes and a few deer. Huge alligators filled the bayous, but the shores were stocked with an abundance of oysters, fish, and turtle. Large numbers of wild ducks and geese wintered there.

Inside the island there was a fairly deep harbor. The bar across the entrance stretching to Point Bolivar sometimes made it difficult to enter. It seldom had more than twelve or fifteen feet of water over it. Pelican Island stood between the island and the mainland. Across the entrance to the bay on Point Bolivar stood the remains of an old mud fort.

On the Galveston side, D'Aure's men had built another mud fort. That was the spot which Jean and Pierre chose for their new home. Lafitte bought out the man whom D'Aure had left in charge of his fort. Six of the former Baratarians met on board one of the schooners in the harbor. They formed a government for the island. Lafitte did not attend the meeting.

"I want them to choose their own officers. However, I do expect them to select me as Governor," Jean said. He knew his men. They knew that he would be the leader. They did not expect anything else; neither did he.

The men formed their government in the name of the Mexican Republic. Under the protection of the Mexican rebels, Lafitte would have an ideal situtation. He could take Spanish prizes without any problems. He was not sure that there really was a Mexican Republic. But an excuse was all that Jean Lafitte needed. The Rebels had provided that excuse.

As Pierre Lafitte said later, "Viva los Mexicanos!" And Jean echoed his thoughts, "Long live the Mexicans!" They were in business again. They could hardly wait to get started. A few prizes would bring in the wealth that they desired.

With several hundred men and enough lumber and tents, Lafitte began his new settlement. By April 5, 1817, he was settled at Galveston. Inside the fort built by D'Aure, Jean Lafitte had a red brick house built. This he promptly named "Maison Rouge" or Red House. Furnished with the rich loot of captured vessels, it was indeed a home fit for the pirate king. Strangers were amazed at the place. The host was certainly handsome and courtly.

To this house Lafitte brought his family, Pierre with his wife Marie Villars, her sister Catherine Villars, and numerous children and slaves. Again the Lafittes had a home.

Other houses were erected for the men. A colony was begun that soon numbered about a thousand men. There were ships chandlers, grocers, saloon keepers, and others who came to supply the needs of the buccaneers.

Business was booming. Lafitte now had a fleet of swift vessels. He had his own ship named *The Pride*. It was a fine brig mounting fourteen guns. He also had an armed small boat painted a beautiful blue, which he called *The Culebra*.

In the year of 1818 Jean and Pierre Lafitte were at the height of their power. Jean named his new establishment "Campeche." The news of Lafitte's Campeche spread among the buccaneers. All those who had prizes to sell made their way to Galveston. Lafitte paid good prices and sold cheaply. He had plenty of trade.

Many captured ships were sunk off Point Bolivar because the pirates did not need them. Their cargoes, however, found a good market across the bay at Galveston. So many slaves were brought in that at times Lafitte sold them at one dollar a pound.

In fact, James Bowie, the inventor of the famous Bowie knife, went to Campeche to buy slaves. He paid an average of one hundred and forty dollars each. Bowie then had a plan to make his purchases legal. He took the slaves to New Orleans. There he managed to have them seized by the authorities. When the government sold them at auction, Bowie bought them back. He managed so well that he made fifty thousand dollars in a year or two.

Lafitte's settlement was planned to be a commune, but without any doubt Jean was the "Bos" of the group. His word was law among the pirates.

"I tell you, man," said one buccaneer, "I wouldn't cross him. No, sir, not unless I absolutely had to do so."

"He's not a man to be taken lightly," answered his companion. "He'd kill you without thinking twice."

"You're right about that, now," answered the first man.

Lafitte did have control of his men. But all was not roses for the Lafittes. Their business was filled with a motley crew. It was indeed a strange scene. Many languages were spoken. When a prize was brought in and divided, there was much celebrating. The booty was divided according to the rank of each man. Woe be to the man who claimed more than his fair share. There was much grumbling among the less fortunate ones. But Lafitte ruled them with an iron hand.

The first "difficulty" that Lafitte had on the island was with the Karankawa Indians. This small but ferocious tribe had been used to spending some time every winter on the island. Now that Lafitte was here, it was not free for them. After a few incidents of stealing from the buccaneers, the Indians were ordered from the island.

Dominique You came to Jean with a report that he had heard.

"Jean, that Italian called Luigi has sneaked an Indian woman into his tent," said Dominique. "I tell you, Jean, I don't like it. He'll cause trouble yet."

Jean sent for the man. He told him flatly that the Indians must be left alone.

"You must take the woman back at once," said Jean. "Her people will be looking for her. They must not find her here. Get her out of here!" Jean's voice was icy.

He would not stand for this kind of trouble among his men. The Indians not only killed their enemies, but they were known to be cannibals on occasion. The buccaneers had too much to lose here. They could not afford Indian troubles. This was the best place in the Caribbean for their operations. No, there was no way that Jean could allow this Indian problem.

Before Jean could enforce his order, the Indians took their revenge. Four men who were out hunting were captured. They were killed by the Indians. When the buccaneers found the bodies, they knew that they had to drive the Indians out for good.

"Pierre, they usually camp at 'Three Trees,' don't they?" asked Jean. "We'll have to take a force and drive them off the island. Otherwise, we'll continue to be bothered. We must get rid of them for good."

Dominique said, "It will have be a good sized force. Those Indians usually have about three hundred braves with them."

"You and Pierre round up about two hundred of the men," answered Jean. "I'll get some men to take down two of the brass cannons from the fort. We'll give them a taste of lead that they won't forget."

The group of pirates overtook the Indians about the center of the island. A fight took place that lasted about three days. Only a few of Lafitte's men were wounded, but they killed about thirty of the Indians. The redmen finally took their canoes and deserted the island.

Lafitte's men had little stomach for Indian fighting.

"I tell you, Beluche," Dominique said to his friend, "This is not for me. I don't like this climbing sand hills and trying to keep an eye out for arrows. It's much easier to get a man swinging from a rope!"

The pirates did not follow the Indians to the mainland. They had had enough of Indian fighting. They felt much better with the sturdy deck of a good brigantine beneath their feet. This Indian fighting was not for them.

The battle became known as the "Battle of Three Trees." From this time on the Indians were a little fearful of the island. They stayed away from Campeche.

IX

Lafitte had other troubles, too. On one occasion a man named Jean Batiste Marotte persuaded Jean to help him pay for a fine felucca that was for sale in New Orleans. Since Marotte and one of his friends, Pepe, could raise only a small sum, Jean agreed to lend him the greater part of the price. The felucca was bought and fitted out for sea. Marotte was put in command with a crew of one hundred and twenty men.

The ship was out of port six months before it met a Spanish ship. At last a sail was seen off the island of Bahia on the Spanish Main. The felucca gave chase. When they got close enough, they discovered that it was an armed Spanish galleon. The Spanish ship was ready for the pirates.

Shouting commands to his men, Marotte ordered out his boarding boats. The Spanish ship opened fire. Five of the pirates were killed. But by clever handling of the boats, they managed to get in under the Spanish guns. They had the ship under their control in a short time.

Marotte ordered his men to put the crew ashore. Some of them grumbled at the waste of time. But they followed the orders.

"The old man's getting soft," said one of the pirates.

"It certainly isn't like it used to be," answered another.

"I don't like this fooling around. There'll likely be another ship in sight before long. It'd be better just to throw them overboard," the first pirate said.

When they had divided the booty from the Spanish ship, Marotte gave Pepe command of the captured Spanish galleon. Then they set out again looking for more prizes. Pepe was an expert seaman. He was really a better commander than Marotee. Through his fine seamanship, they soon took another vessel.

"Man, I didn't think we'd ever make it through that channel," said one seaman, wiping his brow with a dirty scarf.

"You can say what you will," vowed another, "but Pepe surely knows how to push a ship through narrow passes. I guess he's the best "Bos" we've had."

They boarded the captured vessel. This time the cargo was slaves and also some gold plate and jewelry. Marotte was so pleased with his success that he wanted to continue the hunt. But Pepe said that his crew wanted to go into port and divide the booty. However, they had to sell the Negro slaves first. This was done, and then Marotte sent for Pepe to come on board his felucca. There they would divide the spoils.

Unexpectedly one of Pepe's men came to Marotte's ship.

"Pepe asked me to tell you to give his share to your ship's clerk," the man said. "Pepe will take possession of his share when we reach Campeche."

In anger at this short answer, Marotte did not wait to explain to Pepe. He set sail for Galveston. Pepe followed in his own ship.

The good weather favored Pepe's ship. He arrived in Galveston Bay eleven days ahead of Marotte's vessel. Pepe anchored out in the Bay.

Lafitte met the first ship and accompanied Pepe into port. When Marotte's vessel arrived, Pepe and Lafitte boarded Lafitte's *Culebra* to go out to meet Marotte and to bring the felucca into harbor.

Lafitte went with Marotte into the captain's cabin to settle accounts. However, Marotte unfortunately had left an item off his inventory. Probably he intended to keep the gold watches for himself. Lafitte was very angry. Pepe had already told Lafitte about the watches. Lafitte accused Marotte. Marotte, in his anger, spat in Lafitte's face. This was the worst insult he could have made. Lafitte did not kill him on the spot. Instead he challenged Marotte to a duel.

The next day at the appointed time, they rowed across the harbor to Pelican Island, a deserted place where they could have their duel with out anyone's interferring. Lafitte took Pepe in the boat with him.

"Pepe," Jean instructed, "If the worst happens and I fall, you go immediately to my *Pride*. Remain there and hold it until Pierre can get back to Galveston."

"Yes, Bos," answered the frightened Pepe. He could sail with the best of them, but duelling was not his best skill. He feared that Marotte in his anger would kill both of them.

The seconds met the two duellers. They were instructed in the rules of this duel. Jean Lafitte selected his pistol from the two which his second had brought with him. Lafitte walked out to the designated spot and waited for Marotte to take his place.

But before the duel could begin, Marotte surprised the watchers by falling on his knees before Lafitte.

"Bos, Bos," he begged. "Pardon me. I made a bad mistake. I beg you to spare me. For the love of God, spare me!"

He turned coward, begging Lafitte not to shoot him.

Lafitte looked at him in scorn. He granted the pardon, but he cuffed the man's face, pulled his nose, and then kicked a certain part of Marotte's body.

"Now, get out!" ordered Lafitte. "We can do without your kind. Leave the island immediately. Take your property tonight and leave."

Marotte ran for his row boat. His men hurriedly shoved the boat off the shore and made for the island. There Marotte gathered up his belongings, boarded his ship, and sailed away, never to return.

On another occasion Lafitte's crew of the *Pride* decided to mutiny. They had learned that the Spanish authorities were very anxious to get the *Pride*. They would pay a great reward, it was said.

"I tell you, Ramon, we can do it. It'll be more money for all of us than we can get from a few measly prizes," said Carlos. He did not notice Mark edge quietly from the room. Mark was one of those people that others did not notice. In fact, Jean Lafitte had chosen him for that very reason. Unhappily, for the mutineers, he went directly to Jean.

"Bos, Bos," Mark cried as he entered Jean's cabin. "We've got a mutiny on our hands!" He paused for breath. "That bosun's crew think they will take the *Pride*. They want to turn it over to the Spanish authorities in Santo Domingo."

"So they do, do they?" answered an angry Jean. "Well, we'll show them. Call the officers, Mark, and don't let anyone know that we are on their game."

"I certainly won't, Bos," answered the spy. He had been Jean's spy for many months now, and he was proud of his job.

The ship's officer gathered in Jean's cabin. They had their guns ready for the mutineers. When the bosun's crew reached Jean's door, they kicked it in. They expected to take Jean without any trouble. Inside, Jean and his officers began firing. Six of the mutineers were killed at once. The rest changed their minds. They slunk away. Lafitte had his ship under control again.

"Bos, what do we do with these bodies? Do we go ashore to bury them?" asked one of the officers.

"Forget it," answered Jean. "We've had enough trouble now. Just toss them overboard."

"Ay, ay, Bos," said the man.

Later some of the bodies floated up on the beach at Bolivar Point. There some of the other pirates buried them.

Just when everything seemed to be going smoothly for the Lafittes, Fate stepped in. What others could not do, Fate could. In the summer of 1818 a terrific hurricane struck the Gulf of Mexico. The restless waters of the Gulf reflected the steel grey of a sullen sky. The regular murmur of the waves against the beach rose to an angry roar. Higher and higher the long breakers rose against the sandy shore. The ships in the harbor tugged at their anchors.

Confusion took over the settlement. Maria and Catherine watched with fearful eyes as huts and household goods floated past Maison Rouge. Campeche was engulfed. The waves rose and smashed across the island. Many of the people took refuge in the Red House. It occupied the highest point on the land.

Lafitte ordered his men to the ships. They would surely be pounded to pieces on shore if they left them tied up in the bay. They had to be taken out through the channel. There in the open sea they might outlive the storm. At least they had a chance to ride it out. *The Pride* led the other fourteen boats out of the harbor. Shortly they were rocking in safety on the wild, open sea.

"I tell you," said Dominique You. "That Jean Lafitte is really a worker. He was out every minute, trying to take care of the men and their families. I have never seen a man work as hard as he did."

Pierre said, "I know, I know, Dominique. Jean loves Campeche. He would give his life for it."

Jean Lafitte was noble, according to all reports. His first thought was for his men. He strode tirelessly among them, taking care of the sick and wounded. He kept the settlement from being wiped out.

After the flood there were more troubles. The men and their families had to be fed and clothed. Lafitte needed a lot of money in a hurry. He decided upon a bold plan. He sailed to New Orleans. There he secured a loan upon his slaves. Then he sailed back to Campeche with food and clothing for the victims of the flood. He saved the settlement, and with his help the homes were rebuilt.

Campeche never quite got back its former wealth and luxury. It seemed as though the flood had marked the turning of the tide for Campeche. The settlement dropped off. Prizes became harder to get. The Spanish had become more careful. They had lost too many ships to the pirates. Gradually, Spain was taking her shipping out of the Caribbean. Strongly armed vessels protected the ships that did sail in those waters.

Besides the loss of income, the shortage of prizes, Lafitte realized that he was losing control of his men. He did not favor the things that his men were doing.

"Dominique, you know that we cannot attack American ships. Pepe and Manuelo have been going into Louisiana and stealing slaves from the plantations," said Jean. "We can't get away with that kind of business. The United States revenue officers will come here. We can't have that!"

"I know, Jean, but how can we stop them?" asked Dominque. "All of them know what might happen. They just don't seem to care."

"Well, it's bad business. It's not worth the trouble it can bring," answered Jean.

About this time came the case of William Brown. He was a huge, ugly fellow who had come to Texas from New England. He approached Lafitte about taking him into service with the buccaneers. His reputation as a bad man proud of his fame had proceeded him to Galveston.

Pierre said cautiously, "Jean, he's bad news to our

kind of life. We don't need the likes of him."

Dominique You also warned Jean against taking Brown. He feared what Brown might do. Brown was not one who could follow orders from anyone else. But Jean Lafitte liked him.

Lafitte let Brown wait six weeks before he gave him an answer. Finally, he sent Brown out with two vessels.

"Now, Brown, you know that we do not allow the taking of American vessels. We don't want the revenue cutter here checking up on our operations. You stay away from all American shipping," Jean told him firmly.

Brown listened to Lafitte. But when Jean walked away, he snorted that he would show Lafitte what a real pirate could do.

"I'll let him know that I know as much as he does about taking prizes. He's nothing but a land-lubberly milksop. I'll show him," boasted Brown. "I'll bring back prizes that that coward never dreamed of."

Shortly after Brown left Campeche, he met an American vessel, the *Benjamin Hazzard*, near the Sabine river. Unfortunately for Brown, before the pirate could sink the *Hazzard*, the United States revenue schooner, the *Lynx*, appeared. The pirate boats were captured. The pirates took to their small boats. They rowed swiftly toward the shore, and fled into the prairies.

Captain Madison of the *Lynx* found papers on one of the pirate ships. The papers stated that the ship had been commissioned in Galveston on August 20, 1819. With that information, Madison set sail for Galveston to check the truth about the commission.

Brown and his men made their way overland to Galveston. They almost starved to death before they got there. When they arrived at Bolivar Point, they made a fire to signal to Lafitte that they needed help. He sent boats out for the men.

The *Lynx*, battling headwinds, was also making fast for Galveston. Her skipper, Captain Madison, started ashore with fire in his eye. As he neared land, his eye caught a glimpse of a peculiar sight. As he got closer, he saw that it was a gallows that had been built near the beach. From it a corpse was hanging. It was Brown.

Lafitte had kept his promise with Brown. He had called a court together. Brown was tried and convicted. He was sentenced by the court to hang.

For days his body hung there. The pirates felt it was a bad omen for them.

"It turns 'round and 'round," said one of them. "Just watch it. In the day time, he faces toward the sea, but at night he turns and stares at us!"

They stayed away from that part of the beach as long as the body was allowed to hang there. As for Brown's men, Lafitte turned them over to Captain Madison. Madison took them on board the *Lynx* to return with them to New Orleans for trial. Justice was satisfied for the time being.

However, many times the United States was on the point of sending Lafitte and his men packing. But Lafitte had chosen his place on Galveston Island very carefully. He based the settlement between the Sabine and the Colorado rivers. Both Spain and the United States claimed the land between the two rivers.

"You see, Pierre," said Jean. "We can outwit them both. Spain will never let go without a fight. They won't bother us. If the United States can send officers to Galveston, Spain might lose control of it. They'd rather have us there. They'd rather lose a few ships than the whole area of Texas."

"Ay, Jean, ay. It does seem as though we have it for our very own," answered Pierre.

"Surely, Spain will protect us. They want us here," Jean said.

But the Lafittes were not quite right in their thinking. The bad acts of Brown and others upon American shipping were bringing complaints from American citizens. Spain complained to the American government about the pirates. Finally, the United States government decided early in 1821 to send Lieutenant Lawrence Kearney to Galveston in a brig of war, the *Enterprise.*

"Bos, there's a dinghy bound for shore," cried the man on watch. The *Enterprise* was anchored not far from shore. Presently the dinghy came near the shore. Four men landed from the boat. Two officers, handsome in gold braided uniforms and cocked hats, approached the group that stood watching them land.

One of the officers advanced toward the waiting group. He spoke to the first man that he met.

"I am Lieutenant Lawrence Kearney of the United States vessel, the *Enterprise.* I bear a message from my government to Jean Lafitte, now holding Galveston Island." He did not call it Campeche. That was only Jean Lafitte's name for the island. The rest of the nation called it Galveston Island.

"Captain Jean Lafitte at your service," returned the leader of the pirates, motioning his visitors to enter his residence, Maison Rouge. There he opened the papers which they had handed him. He had seated himself at a long table. He gave a curt order to one of his men to bring wine.

Lafitte read the papers slowly and carefully.

"An order to leave the coast at once," he said as he looked up. "Why?"

"The sinking of the *Benjamin Hazzard* a month ago. It was a given and understood agreement that you should not touch the commerce of the United States. You have broken the contract. You must leave," Kearney spoke to Lafitte with a crisp, sure tone.

"But," objected Lafitte, "I did not approve of this attack on your commerce. My orders to Brown—that is, to all my men—are strictly against such a proceeding. These men disobeyed. They were punished. I did not support their act for a moment—nor did I profit by it. This is wrong. Surely you will listen to truth and reason."

Lieutenant Kearney stopped him. "Your pardon, Captain. I was not appointed judge. My orders are to see that you leave Galveston at once."

"I see," returned Jean Lafitte. "But suppose I refuse. I have men, money, guns, ammunition."

Kearney looked at the pirate for a long moment. Then he said coolly, "So has the United States, Captain. Ten thousand to your one!"

Lafitte hit the table with his fingers. "True, it would be but useless sacrifice—and prison perhaps at the end of it."

"Or death," suggested the Lieutenant.

"That would be preferable to prison, sir, indeed," said the island chief shortly.

Lafitte pushed back his chair and arose.

"This is a final order, then—no conditions?" he asked.

"A final order, Sir!" Kearney repeated firmly.

"Very well, then Lieutenant. I bow to the power of the government. By midnight tomorrow we will be ready to leave. I shall give orders at once for the stripping and burning of the settlement," said Lafitte.

Lafitte sent for all of his men to report to the Red House at once. He had Lieutenant Kearney repeat his orders to the men. Without waiting for their comment, Lafitte made known his decision.

"We will leave Campeche at once," he said. "Pierre, you take care of plans for firing the entire settlement. Dominique, you prepare the vessels for sailing. Beluche, you decide which men will go with us. The others are free to make any plans they wish. I will not force any one to go with me. But they must leave the island at once. They cannot stay here."

There was dismay, but not surprise among the men.

"I knew that Brown would bring us trouble," said Dominique. "I told you that when he first came here."

"Ay, Jean," added Pierre. "he was the one who brought us this trouble."

"Lieutenant Kearney, will you do us the pleasure of your company at dinner tonight?" asked Jean to change the direction of the talk.

"I am sorry, but my presence is required on the *Enterprise* tonight," returned Lieutenant Kearney. "My men will want to know the outcome of our talks."

Lafitte watched the men and the boat as they disappeared into the deepening twilight. He turned soberly to look at his Campeche. All was lost. It would have to go. He had lost once again.

The next day all the settlement was ablaze. The Red House, Maison Rouge, was fired last. Jean watched it burn. His eyes were sad. Having found Kearney firm in carrying out his orders, Lafitte placed his goods on board the beautiful *Pride* and sailed away, heading toward the southeast, where he disappeared in the mists.

In planning his departure, Jean had invited Jim Campbell to go with him. Campbell had fought with Perry at the Battle of Lake Erie. He had then drifted to the Sabine river where he had married Sally, the daughter of a ferry-tender. From there he had come to Galveston.

When Sally heard that Lafitte had asked Jim to go with him, she put her foot down. She told Jim what he could do.

"Coil up your rope and anchor right here on shore. You will leave me if you go with Lafitte," she said.

Campbell made his decision. He would stay with Sally.

Lafitte then dug up his treasure, paid off his men, boarded his best brig, and made ready to sail. From Galveston he sailed into the Gulf, cruising about the coast of Yucatan. He met a Spanish vessel laden for the Vera Cruz market. A fight ensued. The Spanish vessel had to strike its colors. The captain offered Lafitte a ransom of one hundred thousand dollars for the ship. The captain was allowed to go to Havana for the money. Bill Chocrane was put on board the prize ship until the Spanish captain returned.

In a short time, instead of the ransom money, the Spanish vessel of war appeared in sight. Lafitte who saw through this plot signaled Cochrane to return to the *Pride*. Cochrane, however, disobeyed Lafitte. He tried to give fight to the Spanish vessel.

Lafitte in the *Pride* set sail. Cochrane was taken without much of a fight. He was imprisoned in Vera Cruz for a long time. However, his bravery was not forgotten. Later he was taken into naval service in Mexico and was made a commodore in the Mexican navy.

Years afterward, a man named Manuel Lopez, claiming to be one of Lafitte's men, told the story of Lafitte's death. He said that Lafitte died in the Yucatan at an Indian town named Silan, about fifteen miles from Merida in 1826. Lafitte was buried in the Campo Santo cemetery of Silan. A tombstone was placed over his grave, Lopez said.

Of Lafitte's men there are some records. Campbell became a good citizen of Galveston, strictly forbidden by his Sally to "out any secrets." Dominique You went back to New Orleans. He went into ward politics and became a respected citizen. He is buried in Old St Louis Cemetery No. 2. His tomb still stands in New Orleans. Beluche, on a certificate from General Jackson, became a commander in the Venezuelan navy. Bill Cochrane, captured by the Spanish, languished in a dungeon for many years, but finally he ended as a Mexican commodore. Pierre Lafitte, presumably, continued his life of piracy until his death sometime in the 1830's.

Jean Lafitte was a pirate, and he was guilty of the blood that his men shed, as well as of the blood he himself had shed with his own hands. But he was by no means wholly devoid of the qualities which to to the making of a hero.

BIBLIOGRAPHY

Barker, Eugene C., "The African Slave Trade in Texas," *Texas Historical Association Quarterly*, October, 1902.

Brindley, Anne A., "Jane Long," *Southwestern Historical Quarterly*, Vol. 56, pp. 220-221.

Bolleart, William, "Life of Jean Lafitte," *United Service Magazine*, October-November, 1851.

Devereux, Mary, *Lafitte of Louisiana*, Boston, Little Brown and Company, 1902.

Harwood, Frances, "Colonel Amasa Turner's Reminiscences of Galveston," *Texas Historical Association Quarterly*, Vol. III, pp. 44-48.

Hunter, Theresa M., "Blood and Booty," *Dallas Morning News*, June 29, 1930 to July 20, 1930. (Clippings mounted in Rosenberg Library, Galveston, Texas.)

Lister, Walter B., "Portrait of a Pirate," *American Mercury* February, 1926, pp. 214-219.

Ramsdell, Charles, Jr., "Why Jean Lafitte Became a Pirate," *Southwestern Historical Quarterly*, Vol. XLIII, April, 1940.

Saxon, Lyle, *Lafitte the Pirate*, New Orleans, Borman House, 1948.

Spears, John B., "Lafitte, the Last of the Buccaneers," *Outing Magazine*, May, 1911, p. 242.

Spears, John B., "The True Story of Lafitte," *Munseys Magazine*, October, 1902, pp. 120-123.

"The Cruise of the *Enterprise*—A Day with Lafitte," *United States Magazine and Democratic Review*, July, 1939.

The Story of Jean and Pierre Lafitte, the Pirate-Patriots, Issued by the Cabildo on Dit, a publication of the Louisiana State Museum.

Thompson, Ray M., *Land of Lafitte, the Pirate*, New Orleans, Borman House, 1948.

Warren, Harris Gaylord, *The Sword Was Their Passport*.